Guide To Legally Selling Hot Sauce

Thomas Robert Thompson

DEDICATION

This book is dedicated to all those who love the stinging, burning sensation of a great hot sauce recipe. Stay spicy my friends!

Table of Contents

Introduction

The hot sauce industry is big business and NOW is the time to get started. Starting a hot sauce business and following legal regulations will put you on track for success.

If you are planning on selling hot sauce in stores or on a large commercial scale than there are several legal things you need to know to follow the proper recipe protection, health guidelines and marketing tactics, without the threat of operations getting shut down or the possibility of fines. You do not need a team of costly lawyers and accountants or large amounts of cash but there are many very important processes to understand the legal aspects of selling hot sauce.

What this book wants to you to avoid

This book wants you to avoid the need to hire a lawyer for your startup hot sauce business or prevent you from starting a business only to be shut down because the proper regulations were not followed.

It will not, however, cover ALL the legal aspects of starting and running a hot sauce business in every part of the world. New policies, laws, and rules are constantly changing with respect to small startup hot sauce businesses, especially on local levels.

The primary reason for not hiring a lawyer during the startup phase of your hot sauce company is that it may be very expensive. This should be taken into consideration if you are entering the hot sauce business on a large scale and producing a considerable amount of sauce each year.

Do's and Don'ts

If you want to sell your brand of hot sauce there are several common principles that need to be followed to ensure you are **making, selling, and marketing your hot sauce without running into legal issues** that could shut down business.

Do

Protect your recipe with a trade secret, find a commercial kitchen to make sauce or register a manufacturing facility with the FDA and label sauce without any misconception or mislabeling. This will require local regulations and inspections in the state and county that you live in to obtain a license to sell sauce across the country.

95% of hot sauce companies use a Co-Packer to manufacture their hot sauce recipes

Don't

Don't start making mass quantities of hot sauce without first setting yourself up for success. That is what this book is for. Don't make a couple small batch hot sauces and sell to a couple of friends...go big time! Manufacture hot sauce yourself or hire someone to do it for you, produce large quantities, and sell, sell, sell!

Make a great hot sauce and protect it

I mention this in just about every book I write but a strong and successful hot sauce business begins with a great hot sauce recipe. This could be Gramma's recipe, a new recipe invented by you, a recipe purchased, or a recipe that has been used in many commercial hot sauce products.

The only thing "legal" you need to understand and consider about making hot sauce is if you are using someone else's recipe (there is no copyright law to protect recipes) and what you are going to do with it. You can steal it...but don't. It is unethical and the competitor's sauce will most likely be better than yours if they are a successful manufacturer of sauce. If you have a recipe from another hot sauce manufacturer (they are kind of publicly known) you shouldn't use it to sell your own sauce. You can sell someone else's hot sauce, legally, under contract manufacturing but so will every other brand that has used the same sauce.

However, there are circumstances in the hot sauce industry where you can legally sell someone else's hot sauce recipe. This gives you limited control over the content but full control over the labeling, packaging, branding, and marketing campaign. A successful hot sauce business focuses on the core of the product…a great recipe! **<u>Your sauce should be original.</u>**

Two parts of a recipe

Any hot sauce recipe can be broken down into two main parts of a recipe: **the ingredients and the process.** Although this statement makes hot sauce seem as though it is a simple product, and it is in many ways compared to other types of food…the process in which it is made makes it a very complex product.

The main contents or ingredients of hot sauce are usually nothing more than hot peppers, some type of liquid such as vinegar, citrus juice or water, and some spices.

Legal recipe

Don't worry... there isn't any such term, "legal recipe", in the hot sauce business, or any business.

There isn't much to be concerned about legally as it is associated with a recipe. There have been lawsuits over recipes, but they are usually specific to the process, directions, and instructions on how to make it or the **Trade Secret** used. Instead of using an existing recipe with hopes that there isn't much competition...invent your own!

<u>Be original, invent your own hot sauce recipe</u>. It's the process that is just as important as the ingredients in a hot sauce recipe. This process is called a Trade Secret, and it will hold up better in court than not having one if your hot sauce recipe is being used by a competitor.

Manufacturers of hot sauce that use complex processes like fermentation, ingredient formulas, or processes that have many steps will precisely document the process and will usually have any employees sign off on their secrecy, literally. These files are then kept under a lock and key so the "secret" is not exposed.

Trade Secret

Be particular about breaking down the steps to include everything that is done in preparing and making a hot sauce.

This does not need to include shopping for ingredients or selecting the proper produce vendor once you are producing on a large scale, but the source of the product is important.

However, <u>include steps like cutting hot peppers or leaving them whole</u>. This seems trivial but if the next step is fermenting a mash or roasting whole peppers then this will make a difference in the outcome of the sauce. These steps will need to be documented in a **Trade Secret** or **Scheduled Process** (in some areas) and will set your recipe apart from the competition.

Write down everything that you are doing to prepare for and make a hot sauce as if you were giving someone directions. You can always eliminate what is repeated or what is not necessarily part of the recipe or Trade

Secret later. Keep in mind details that may include (but not limited to) blender speed, cooking temperature, fermentation duration, or order in which the ingredients are combined. The recipe process should be detailed and specific as possible.

A recipe process should be detailed and specific as possible

For example, if you are fermenting, the next step is important and needs to be detailed. This will include duration, container type, and storage temperature as well as other details.

We do not need to go into any more detail on writing down each step…you get the idea. If you only have 2 to 3 steps…it may not be a Trade Secret.

Trade Secret Checklist

The process of making your hot sauce recipe should be carefully documented step by step but consider some other detailed information to

include as well.

The process of making your hot sauce recipe should be carefully documented step by step but consider some other detailed information to include as well. Some of this may have already been included in the process but any details will support originality.

List of ingredients and weight?   Yes ☐   No ☐

Does process include formulas?   Yes ☐   No ☐

Do you have the bill of sales?   Yes ☐   No ☐

Is there a flow chart?   Yes ☐   No ☐

Was machinery used?   Yes ☐   No ☐

A Trade Secret can protect a hot sauce recipe if it is original, provides a commercially valuable product, is not in the public area and reasonable efforts have been made to maintain its confidentiality.

Is the process secret?   Yes ☐ No ☐

Here is an example: Blending is not a secret. Nor is
chopping but blending at a certain speed for a distinct
duration is. So is chopping hot peppers to a certain
consistency, mushiness, or texture. Also, if your process
includes roasting for a certain duration at a certain
temperature and including salts or spices then it is a
secret. Add steps or ingredients to make a hot sauce
unique.

Is the process valuable?   Yes ☐ No ☐

All hot sauce is valuable right? Another term that could
be used for valuable is **unique or enhances an
otherwise bland meal**. Gluten-free, fat-free, and sugar-
free all make a condiment stand out. Is your hot sauce
fat-free or sugar-free...that's valuable!

Is process known in the industry?   Yes ☐ No ☐

Everyone in the hot sauce industry knows that hot

peppers are blended into a hot sauce, but they may not know how long and at what speed to create a specific texture. There are other more complex processes such as aging and smoking that are common, but each process for each recipe can be unique.

Is the process obvious to others?   Yes ☐   No ☐

There is nothing obvious about making a great-tasting hot sauce. It is a combination of special ingredients created in a way that only you know. Consider the uniqueness of the process when you make your sauce.

It is OK to check no to some of these boxes but that means your sauce may not be as original to become a Trade Secret. You should document in any way to help protect what you have worked so hard on and keep the process under lock and key.

Documenting recipe creations can legally protect your recipe creations

"Stealing" a recipe

Recipes, or what most refer to as the ingredients, are openly printed on all hot sauce bottles... but processes are not.

Over the course of its inception as a condiment hot sauce has probably seen a thousand different recipes to include the many colors and consistencies that hot sauce is today. Some of them are very similar and there are others that stand out.

A standard, classic, or traditional hot sauce recipe like a Louisiana hot sauce has just a few standard ingredients; aged peppers, vinegar, garlic, and salt but there are close to 100 on the market.

These sauces are not stealing each other's recipe, but use **different processes** that create completely different flavors.

How copyright DOES NOT protect a recipe

In general, recipes themselves are not eligible for copyright protection because copyright law typically does not protect facts, ideas, systems, or methods of operation.

In general, recipes themselves are not eligible for copyright protection because copyright law typically does not protect facts, ideas, systems, or methods of operation. However, the specific expression of a recipe, such as the wording, arrangement, and creative elements in a cookbook or a recipe blog, may be eligible for copyright protection. This means that the way a recipe is written, the accompanying photographs, and any creative elements added to the presentation could be protected by copyright.

A copyright protects the specific expression of an idea, not the idea itself. Therefore, if someone were to write their own unique description of a recipe or create original illustrations or photographs to accompany it, like a hot sauce cookbook, those specific creative elements could be protected by copyright.

Document your hot sauce recipe

If you have a special hot sauce recipe... and I know you do... document everything.

If you have a sauce that you make from a recipe you have held onto in your head document it as your Trade Secret on an electronic file, PDF, Excel spreadsheet or Word doc. A trade secret will be held up in court as a legal document only if you precisely log the process your hot sauce undergoes during production. According to nolo.com the Trade Secret needs to follow two principles:

1. The manner in which the hot sauce is made gives it a competitive advantage.
2. The process or information used to make the hot sauce is done in secrecy.

You may think that creating a document instead of keeping a recipe in your head will give you a better chance of getting hold of the recipe and duplicating it but it is this documented process that verifies it is yours. Take these important steps when you have finally perfected your sauce and find a great establishment to mass produce it.

United States Patented and Trademark

The United States Patented and Trademark Office (USPTO) has lots of additional information of protecting a Trade Secret.

This office will also handle the registration of a **Trademark** but that is not necessarily related to your recipe. A Trademark protects your logo or phrase used in marketing. Search the Trademark Electronic Search System (TESS) to find if your logo is unique.

There is another process of protecting your hot sauce recipe and that is with a patent. It could be difficult, time consuming and costly to patent a recipe but it can be done. Once you have legally protected your hot sauce recipe it is now time to find a location to produce it.

Keep track of your hot sauce creations

Creating new hot sauce recipes in the kitchen can be a science and if you don't carefully document your creations…a great hot sauce recipe can be lost and forgotten forever. I am always experimenting with different recipes to create an original hot sauce and often fail to log what I have done…and the recipe is lost forever.

This can be as easy as writing down all the ingredients of your hot sauce to include the quantities by weight. It is important to note the recipe quantities by weight because this will be the labeling requirements by the jurisdiction regulating the labeling requirements just about **anywhere in the world.** This list is different from the Trade Secret and will be the primary information to be included on the nutritional label of your hot sauce.

Now that you have managed all your great hot sauce recipes it's time to mass produce them.

Making the sauce

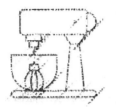

There are four primary agencies that provide food safety regulations in the United States and elsewhere and this applies directly to manufacturing hot sauce.

The Food and Drug Administration, Department of Health and Human Services, Food Safety Inspection Services & US Department of Agriculture all have very similar standards pertaining to preparing and producing food products for sale.

There is no reason to NOT follow food manufacturing guidelines when making hot sauce. If you intend to sell hot sauce on a global level, then it is very difficult to legally avoid adhering to food safety standards established in your area. If you intend to sell hot sauce at a local level such as farmer's market, you are still legally obligated to provide a safe product to consumers.

Food and Drug Administration

The FDA does regulate hot sauce production. The FDA

mandates that makers of hot sauce adhere to good manufacturing principles, FDA-approved ingredients, and strict labeling standards to ensure safety, quality, and proper labeling of the product. Additionally, hot sauce producers are required to provide accurate information and comply with food safety requirements.

FDA regulates hot sauce production by requiring certain labeling and safety standards. According to the information available, the FDA mandates that hot sauce labels include the product name, net weight, manufacturing information, nutritional data, and allergen information. The ingredients must be listed in order of weight, and the label should include the name and address of the manufacturer, packer, or distributor.

Additionally, the FDA requires that the pH of hot sauce must be less than 4.6 and an acid, such as vinegar, should be added to ensure this. The hot sauce should also be brought to a boil to destroy any potential pathogens.

Department of Health and Human Services

The Department of Health and Human Services (HHS) doesn't directly control hot sauce production. The regulation of hot sauce production falls under the jurisdiction of the Food and Drug Administration (FDA), which is an agency within the HHS. The FDA sets and enforces standards for the production, labeling, and safety of hot sauce and other food products to ensure consumer safety and product quality.

The Department of Health and Human Services (HHS) does have a role in regulating local food businesses, particularly through its agency, the Food and Drug Administration (FDA). The FDA is responsible for regulating the safety and labeling of food products, including those produced by local food businesses. Additionally, the Centers for Disease Control and Prevention (CDC), which is part of the HHS, plays a role in preventing foodborne illnesses and impacts the food industry through its efforts to strengthen regulations and policies for food safety.

Food Safety Inspection Services

The Food Safety and Inspection Agency is a Canadian government agency responsible for safeguarding food, animals, and plants, which enhances the health and well-being of Canada's people, environment, and economy. It ensures that Canada's food supply is safe, accessible, and sustainable.

US Department of Agriculture

If you are manufacturing and selling hot sauce on a domestic level, then there will be local agencies that govern over these federal regulations. This will be your local agricultural department having jurisdiction.

Find a kitchen to make sauce on a commercial or semi commercial scale

The difficulties of understanding the legal implications of registering a kitchen, either in your home or commercially, are that laws, regulations, and inspections by the department of health are different from state to state. These policies may also be different between counties within the state and will certainly be different between each country. Working from home is convenient and less expensive than renting or leasing kitchen space but some of these smaller kitchens, which would be less expensive for a startup business, may not provide for a large-scale operation and may not qualify per local jurisdictions.

Currently only about half of the states in the US allow hot sauce that is made in a home-based kitchen to be sold directly to consumers and many of these states require the sauce to be below the FDA recommended pH level of 4.6. Decisions on selling on a global level or within smaller more defined regions need to be made to set up your business model.

Setting up sales for success

The last thing you want to do is make and bottle a great hot sauce only to have business shut down because you didn't provide the correct sanitary conditions or follow the proper inspection protocols.

Setting up a kitchen space

Setting up a kitchen space needs to take into consideration two things: **do you intend to sell your hot sauce globally or do you wish to sell your hot sauce domestically within your region?** This decision will determine how you set up your kitchen space to make and produce hot sauce.

Setting up operations to sell hot sauce can have two options to focus on: selling on the global level and selling on the local level. Each of these will have completely different legal implications. This can be defined simply that **selling hot sauce on a global level requires much more stringent legal actions and selling on a local level**

may not. Although selling on a local level will certainly have rules and regulations to follow, they may not be as complex or rigorous as selling hot sauce around the world.

Setting up to sell globally

Setting up your hot sauce business to sell anywhere around the world means that you need to follow food and safety regulations that are recognized globally such as the FDA, DHHS, FSIS, & USDA.

Setting up your hot sauce business to sell anywhere around the world means that you need to follow food and safety regulations that are recognized globally.

This still means that there may be some local permits and licensing required. My advice would be to **find a co-packer who can produce and package your sauce for sale through global ecommerce channels.**

Examples of selling globally

1. Making hot sauce in a licensed facility and selling through online retailers
2. Placing your branding image on a private label bottle and distributing it to other countries
3. Getting a product on store shelves with international locations

Setting up to sell locally

Establishing a hot sauce business locally means that you may be following much less stringent laws and requirements. It also means that there could be restrictions on the type of hot sauce you can sell, where you are selling it, and the amount of money you can make annually.

Examples of selling locally

1. Farmer's markets
2. Stands
3. Restaurants
4. Local bodega
5. Independently owned shops

Pros and Cons of selling globally / locally

Selling hot sauce globally

Pro

- Opens up opportunities for huge sales
- Lots of demand for new hot sauces
- Hot sauce industry is on the rise

Con

- Can take a long time for brand image
- Higher expenses then selling locally

Selling hot sauce locally

Pro

- Fairly easy entry level approach
- Good for entrepreneurship
- Not a huge financial commitment

Con

- There is usually a sales cap on annual earnings
- Not all jurisdictions allow the sale of hot sauce under local laws

Commercial kitchen vs home kitchen

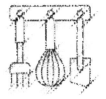

The end results of your kitchen space will be the same... bottled hot sauce! However, the regulations you need to follow will be very different.

Find and set up a kitchen for commercial operations

Some local authorities may restrict the use of home kitchens on a commercial scale so you may need to find some other options like sharing or renting. Regulations such as Article 20-C Food Processor Establishment License (NYS) require the kitchen space or any area where processing and other food manufacturing takes place to be licensed. This could be a long and costly process and will put a lot of the legal responsibilities on you. Read below on renting or sharing kitchens to bypass some of these regulations.

Some facilities may be exempt from the need to apply for this type of permit if food is processed in the home. This exemption is called a **Home Processor Exemption,** and it usually pertains to those selling at farmers markets, craft fairs or farm stands and not someone who wants to sell hot sauce in stores at the commercial level.

NASDA

The National Association of State Departments of Agriculture (NASDA) can help you locate the Department of Agriculture in your jurisdiction. They have a state directory for all 50 states in the US where you can find out about the licensing requirements that you may need to register or license a kitchen in your area.

Find your local health department to get your kitchen inspected

This is one of the most important steps to abide by if you plan on entering the hot sauce market if you already own or rent an established kitchen.

Because this information is different from state to state or within every county within that state, it is difficult to acknowledge exact information in this article. Because these sites are different from each other and overloaded with information, it may be difficult to navigate through to find the information that pertains to you.

Contact local health officials in your state. Email your questions to the contact in the state in which you will be manufacturing the food. The **Directory of State and Local Officials** will direct you to a local official who will usually be under the title of Agriculture and Markets.

This site will prompt you to a directory of names with the contact information. The far-left column will give you the areas that they govern. Copy the email on the far right and then send a form letter. You will most likely get a return e mail without a direct answer, but it will include other pertinent contact information.

Your kitchen will have to pass inspection

Nacho.org (National Association of County Health Officials) has links to health inspectors in every state in the US. I found the local health department in my county in just a few minutes. They will usually have a phone number and e mail contact number.

Home Processor Exception

In many states a **Home Processor Exemption** allows hot sauce to be packaged in your home and are to be sold only in your state. In my state of NY hot sauce falls under the prohibited foods to be manufactured and sold under a Home Processor Exemption therefore a licensed facility is needed but this is not the case in every state or every region in the world.

Kitchen space on a budget

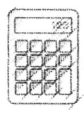

If you have purchased this book, then you are probably just starting out and have a limited budget.

Incubator kitchen (shared kitchen)

Sharing kitchen space is not unusual for startup hot sauce companies. Aside from the requirements below, a basic commercial kitchen will have some equipment, utensils, storage, and workspace. If you have been making hot sauce for any length of time this will be obvious to you. There are many regulations, inspections, and associated costs with obtaining and running a commercial kitchen on your own. One way to bypass some of the legal requirements is to **rent kitchen space** from an establishment that has the permits and inspections already obtained. These are called "incubator" kitchens.

If you are not ready to invest in the real estate of owning a commercial kitchen then you need a kitchen either owned, rented, leased, or shared. The form in the example above calls a "shared kitchen" a **Kitchen Incubator Food Processing Establishment**. This will allow you to bypass many of the legal implications of owning your own kitchen and will shift it to another owner. Although there may often be contractual agreements such as a lease. Many kitchens function like this and may have several processed foods using some of the same equipment but this is a common occurrence for a startup hot sauce business.

If you are new or inexperienced at making hot sauce, then here is a list of items you may require to make and store your hot sauce in a shared kitchen space or incubator kitchen. This is not a complete list of what a commercial kitchen needs to fully function as a manufacturing facility. Make a list similar to the one below to define exactly what your needs would be for an incubator kitchen.

1. Hot / cold water
    A. Having both hot and cold water is a necessity.
    B. Multiple sinks are nice to have.
2. Hours of availability
    A. Quite possibly you are renting or sharing kitchen space.
    B. When is it available?
3. Space for commercial blender or use of a blender
    A. Being able to use a blender and not carry one in and out is a plus.
4. Storage for peppers
    A. Some ingredients may need special storage conditions like refrigeration.
5. Countertop space

A. The proper countertop space is essential.

6. Cleaning products
    A. This could be an extra cost.
7. Storage for your bottled sauce
    A. There may not be storage available once your sauce is bottled.
8. Basic utensils
    A. It would be nice not having to carry equipment in and out, regardless of how small things like utensils can be.
9. Containers for mixing
    A. The more equipment you can use, and the less you bring in and out is best.
10. Large cooking pots
11. Walk in cooler

Make a site visit

You probably should not make any commitment without first visiting the location. This will give you a good idea of the layout and conditions.

Use an existing kitchen

Some of the same items above may be desired if you are renting kitchen space but more often than not will not be available even using an existing kitchen space. The use of specific items can be determined between you and the owner of the space.

Rent kitchen space

Renting kitchen space that has already passed all inspections is a great option for someone entering the hot sauce business. Renting space may not provide some of the same amenities such as the use of equipment like an incubator kitchen may. The Kitchen Door is a service that can introduce you to local kitchens. I found one in my area for $22 an hour with a countertop to invite guests and test sauces.

Commercial Kitchens for Rent is like the Kitchen Door. If this is the option, you plan on following consider pricing and access. This site allows you to search for commercial kitchens for rent by state.

The only legal requirement would be the agreement between you and the owner and it is extremely important to have this...in writing. Like the other permits, inspections and licenses the local government entity will be different depending on location.

Questions to ask renting kitchen space

1. **What hours or times of the week are available?**
2. **Is there a lease or rental agreement?**
3. **What are the monthly costs?**
4. **Is there equipment available for use?**
5. **Are there storage capabilities?**

Kitchen requirements checklist

Shared use kitchen operator responsibilities

This is the person licensed under the Department of Agriculture to process food under Article 20-C. Again, article 20-C is NYS and the requirements for the kitchen owner may be different in each state or country as stated previously.

The operator needs to obtain this license before they can allow you to rent or lease the space. Locate a kitchen so you can use this space without the legalities of inspections, insurance, permits and other local requirements.

Here is what to look for from the operator of a shared kitchen. These items would be 100% necessary to avoid any legal implications associated with a licensed kitchen. These items should be discussed and verified before any contracts are signed or any money is exchanged.

1. Copies of health inspection records.
2. What storage is available?
3. Does it help with permits?
4. Are there any kitchen consultants?

There can be some limitations such as availability and use for an incubator kitchen. Eventually as sales increase you will want to invest in owning your own space. This can become a commitment and can increase the costs of your operations.

Operating your own commercial kitchen

Owning and operating a commercial kitchen can allow a lot of freedom in the hours you operate and can become a great area to practice the art of different hot sauce recipes. However, one of the downsides would be the cost associated with owning and operating a facility. Operating these kitchens will bring us back to obtaining inspections and will also be the costliest venture.

1. Find a location
2. Arrange an inspection

These two simple steps are much more involved than what this book can encompass. Locating a commercial kitchen can be done through local restate agents and your inspections will be done locally as well.

Registration of a food facility

Registering a facility with the FDA needs to be done if you are manufacturing food in a facility. It is the facility that will need to meet the FDA's criteria. These regulations may be different by state and will also be different if you are selling hot sauce directly from a physical establishment. Other organizations worldwide may regulate food manufacturing facilities differently. Retail food businesses and farmers markets do not need to register with the FDA.

Some facilities are exempt from needing to register but it is necessary if you plan on manufacturing hot sauce on a commercial scale by selling in stores, both physical and online.

FDA registration requirements

Registering with the FDA includes a stable and secure environment in which your hot sauce is manufactured and processed. This includes regular record keeping, inspections and reporting if there is cause for irregular methods of manufacturing that could cause illness.

Registration will include, name of the establishment, principal place of business, the location of each establishment in which that processing is carried out, the processing method and a list of foods processed in each establishment.

Title 21 CFR 114 (Code of Federal Regulations)

Title 21 CFR 114 refers to the Code of Federal Regulations title that pertains to acidified foods like many hot sauces. It outlines the regulations to produce acidified foods, including the processing, packing, and distribution of such products. These regulations are designed to ensure the safety and proper handling of acidified foods to protect public health.

Hot sauce falls under Title 21 CFR 114 Acidified Foods / Low Acidified Canned Foods if the pH is below 4.6. You can find this file on the Federal Food and Drug Administration's web site fda.org. This site can be very difficult to navigate through but has all the information you are looking for.

Apply for a Food Service Establishment Permit

Food Service Establishment Permits are obtained if hot sauce is processed and sold within a restaurant, sandwich shop or other retail food service locations.

Some homemade foods such as baked goods, jellies and sauces can qualify for a Home Processor Exemptions. If you are pursuing larger operations like a commercial establishment than you will have to go through the Department of Agriculture and Markets in your state.

USDA Food Standards and Labeling Policy Book

This document is a glossary of terms in dictionary form and can be very useful for the knowledge of making and producing hot sauce. This is a large document with many definitions referring to meats but there are some items that would include the contents of hot sauce or a claim on your label that your sauce includes these products.

For example, products labeled "hickory smoked" must provide certification that 100% hickory is used in the smoking process. Review the Food Standards and Label Policy Handbook from the USDA.

How can I sell sauce in different regions?

Selling hot sauce within local regions, within state lines for example, is easier and less costly than selling outside of those regions or across jurisdictions.

All food offered for sale in interstate commerce needs to adhere to the US Department of Agriculture or better known as the USDA. This includes the safety and handling of the process packaging and proper labeling. Current Good Manufacturing Practice (CGMP) (21 Code of Federal Regulations (CFR) Part 110). This is another guide from the FDA that covers sanitary conditions, equipment handling and good manufacturing practices.

The manufacture of food and food products will be governed by local entities but as you decide to sell outside of your region other governmental agencies like the USDA will give approval. All food intended for interstate commerce (any transactions across state borders) is regulated by the FDA.

Do I need to follow FDA?

Yes. This is an agency that regulates food manufacturing, processing, nutritional contents, and packaging in the US. Regulations will be different in your jurisdiction in which you are manufacturing and selling sauce.

If you are manufacturing and selling hot sauce in another country, you must follow FDA guidelines to legally import hot sauce to the USA for the purpose of physical sales. The hot sauce will be subject to any inspections at the port of entry.

FDA District Office

As stated several times in this book, some areas where the manufacturing of hot sauce takes place will have local authorities working out of local offices. The offices under the FDA that perform all field activities are called the **Office of Regulatory Affairs (ORA).** This is the organization that will perform the inspections of your registered facility.

A home-based business doesn't apply to federal regulations, but we are going big here and want to make sales across the country and eventually globally. Right? Check your local county health agencies for these regulations. Only acidified hot sauces in about half of the United States qualify as a home-based business.

Hot sauce business models

How to get away with <u>not</u> registering a food manufacturing facility (All legally!)

There are five ways to enter the hot sauce business and not all of them have similar legal requirements. **On Demand, Drop Shipping, Private Label, Co-Packing and Bottle Your Own** are all business models used in the hot sauce industry. Of these business models Private Labeling and Co-Packing do not require YOU to register a kitchen facility. That is because these two business models offer an opportunity to have YOUR hot sauce manufactured in a facility that is owned, leased, or registered by someone else.

On Demand

"On-demand" typically refers to a service or system where users can access or receive something immediately when they need it. This concept is prevalent in various industries and technologies. Here are a few contexts where "on-demand" is commonly used:

In essence, "on-demand" is about providing goods, services, or information immediately and as needed, often facilitated by technology and the internet. It reflects a shift towards more flexible and user-centric models of consumption.

Drop Shipping

In the hot sauce industry, Drop shipping focuses on the business side of things and not necessarily the making hot sauce side of things. If you have culinary experience and are all about getting your hands dirty inside of a kitchen space, then a drop shipping business model may not be for you.

Drop shipping is a retail fulfillment method where a store doesn't keep the products it sells in stock. Instead, when a store sells a product using the drop shipping model, it purchases the item from a third party and has it shipped directly to the customer. As a result, the merchant (you running a hot sauce business) never sees or handles the product.

Here's how a drop shipping process for a hot sauce business typically works:

1. Customer places an order. A customer places an order on the retailer's online store.

2. Order forwarded to the supplier.

3. The retailer then purchases the product from a third-party supplier (usually a wholesaler or manufacturer) and provides the supplier with the customer's details and shipping address.

4. Supplier ships the product. The supplier ships the product directly to the customer.

The key advantages of drop shipping include:

Low upfront costs

Since the retailer doesn't have to purchase inventory upfront, there are lower initial costs compared to traditional retail models.

Reduced risk

The risk of unsold inventory is minimized because the retailer only purchases the product when they make a sale.

Easier to start

Setting up an online store and starting a drop shipping business is often quicker and requires less capital than establishing a traditional retail store.

However, there are also challenges and considerations:

Lower profit margins

Since the retailer is buying products at a higher price (per unit) than they would in bulk, profit margins can be lower.

Less control over inventory and shipping

Because the retailer doesn't handle the products, there's less control over inventory levels and the shipping process. This can lead to issues such as backorders and shipping delays.

Dependence on suppliers

The success of a drop shipping business is closely tied to the reliability and efficiency of the chosen suppliers.

Drop shipping has become a popular model for entrepreneurs entering the e-commerce space, especially for those looking to start a business with minimal investment and risk.

Private label

For a private label hot sauce business model, you don't legally own the recipe, but you do own everything associated with the branding.

A private label hot sauce business involves creating and selling hot sauce products under your own brand name rather than selling a pre-existing, established brand. Here's a breakdown of the key components of a private label hot sauce business:

Product Development

In a private label hot sauce business, you typically work with a manufacturer or a hot sauce producer to develop a unique hot sauce recipe that will be sold under your brand. This may involve selecting specific ingredients, determining the level of spiciness, and creating a flavor profile that distinguishes your hot sauce from others in the market.

Branding

You create your own brand for the hot sauce, including designing a logo, packaging, and marketing materials. This allows you to establish a distinct identity for your products.

Manufacturing and Packaging

Once the recipe and branding are established, you work with a manufacturer to produce the hot sauce in bulk. The manufacturer also assists in packaging the product according to your brand specifications.

Private Labeling

The manufacturer often provides a "white label" or "private label" service, where they produce the hot sauce with your branding, image, graphics, logo, and packaging. This allows you to focus on marketing and selling the product without the need to handle the production process.

Distribution and Sales

You can sell your private label hot sauce through various channels, such as online platforms, local retailers, or specialty stores. Building relationships with distributors and retailers may also be part of your strategy to expand the reach of your hot sauce.

Marketing and Promotion

As with any business, marketing plays a crucial role. You need to create awareness of your brand and hot sauce products through online marketing, social media, advertising, and other promotional activities.

Private label businesses offer entrepreneurs the opportunity to enter a market with their own branded products without the need to develop the entire production process from scratch.

It allows for customization and differentiation in a competitive market. The success of the business often depends on the quality of the product, effective branding, and a well-executed marketing strategy.

Co-Packing

Co-packing, short for contract packing or co-manufacturing, refers to the business arrangement where one company (the co-packer) provides packaging services for another company's products (your hot sauce business). In this arrangement, the company that owns the product outsources the packaging process to a specialized third-party provider.

Co-packing is a common practice in various industries, including food and beverage, pharmaceuticals, cosmetics, and consumer goods. **Many top performing successful hot sauce businesses use this model.**

Packaging Services

Co-packers typically offer a range of services related to packaging, including product assembly, labeling, packing, and sometimes even distribution. The co-packer may have specialized equipment and expertise to efficiently handle the packaging process. For some companies you may just have to provide the hot sauce recipe.

Cost Efficiency

Companies often opt for co-packing to benefit from cost savings. Co-packers can leverage economies of scale, expertise, and specialized equipment to streamline the packaging process, reducing costs you may have trying to bottle your own.

Expertise and Specialization

Co-packers are often specialists in packaging processes. They may have advanced technology, skilled personnel, and knowledge of regulatory requirements. This expertise allows the product owner to focus on their core competencies, such as product development and marketing.

Flexibility

Co-packing provides flexibility in production and packaging volume. Businesses can scale their production without significant capital investment in equipment or facilities. This is particularly advantageous for companies with fluctuating demand or seasonal products.

Regulatory Compliance

Co-packers are often well-versed in industry regulations and compliance standards and will typically have fully inspected facilities. This can be crucial, especially in industries with strict regulations. Working with a co-packer can help ensure that products meet all necessary quality and safety standards.

Reduced Risk

Co-packing can reduce the risk for product owners by transferring certain responsibilities to a specialized partner. This includes risks associated with equipment maintenance, labor management, and changes in production volume.

Private Labeling

Co-packers may offer private labeling services, allowing companies to sell products under their own brand without the need for extensive in-house manufacturing capabilities.

While co-packing offers numerous advantages, companies should carefully select a reliable and reputable co-packer to ensure quality, consistency, and adherence to specifications. Clear communication and well-defined agreements are essential to a successful co-packing relationship.

Legal Obligations

It's important for both the product owner (brand owner) and the co-packer to clearly define these obligations to avoid disputes and ensure compliance with relevant laws and regulations.

The legal obligations of co-packing agreements can vary depending on the terms negotiated between the parties involved. However, there are some common legal considerations and obligations that are typically addressed in co-packing contracts.

Quality Standards and Specifications

The co-packer is usually obligated to meet specific quality standards and product specifications outlined in the contract. This includes adherence to regulatory requirements and any industry standards applicable to the products being co-packed.

Intellectual Property Rights

The agreement should address issues related to intellectual property, including trademarks, copyrights, and any proprietary information. It should define the rights and responsibilities of each party regarding the use of intellectual property in the packaging and marketing of the products.

Regulatory Compliance

Co-packers are often responsible for ensuring that the packaging process complies with relevant laws and regulations. This may include food safety regulations, labeling requirements, and other industry-specific standards.

Confidentiality and Non-Disclosure

Both parties usually have a mutual interest in protecting sensitive information. Co-packing agreements often include provisions for confidentiality and non-disclosure to prevent the unauthorized sharing of proprietary information.

Liability and Indemnification

The contract should clearly outline each party's liability in case of product defects, recalls, or other issues. Indemnification clauses may be included to specify which party is responsible for covering costs associated with legal claims or damages.

Insurance Requirements

Co-packers may be required to maintain specific types and amounts of insurance coverage, including liability insurance, to protect both parties in the event of accidents, product recalls, or other unforeseen incidents.

Production Timelines and Delivery

The agreement should specify production timelines, delivery schedules, and any penalties for delays. Clear expectations for order quantities and lead times are crucial to avoid disruptions in the supply chain.

Dispute Resolution

The contract should include a mechanism for resolving disputes, such as through mediation or arbitration, to avoid costly legal battles.

Termination Clauses

The agreement should outline the conditions under which either party can terminate the contract. This includes provisions for early termination, breach of contract, or other specified circumstances.

Compliance with Employment Laws

If the co-packer employs personnel, the agreement should address compliance with labor and employment laws, including worker safety, wage and hour regulations, and other relevant standards.

It's essential for both parties to consult with legal professionals experienced in contract law and industry-specific regulations to ensure that the co-packing agreement is comprehensive, fair, and legally sound. Legal advice can help mitigate risks and protect the interests of all parties involved.

Hiring a Co-Packer

Hire the <u>right</u> co-packer for <u>your</u> hot sauce business.

Consider the following points to be discussed with companies you are considering as a co-packing partner. Know what you are getting into before any contracts are signed.

1. **Do you bottle hot sauce?** - Many companies may co-pack sauces but not hot sauce or they have grown their business to include the demand for new sauces being created.

2. **Know the recipe ingredients** - If you are using your Grandma's hand-me-down recipe, make sure you have the ingredients and amounts listed somewhere...in detail. This will probably include much more information than you have documented and may take several trial runs.

3. **Have a detailed description of the process** - Is the recipe fermented, roasted or does it involve other complex processing? This is just as important as the ingredients.

4. **What is the largest batch produced?** - The co-packer may have to manipulate the recipe slightly when it gets mass produced. What size batch do you typically produce?

5. **Initial startup costs** - Every customer is different but discussing the costs upfront could be a deciding factor in your decision. They should be able to provide estimate figures.

6. **Provide sample** - You will need to provide samples to the co-packer, and they may need to be shipped if you are not within travel distance.

7. **Contract signing** - No contract means no commitment. Larger companies may have a minimal order amount and need a signed contract before further consultation.

8. **Label design** - If you already have a label design most co-packers will work with that. There will be additional costs for the label application.

9. **Can I provide my own label?** - This will depend on the company because the physical label may not work with their machinery and equipment.

10. **Recipe control** - This is what co-packing is. If you don't have control or recipe creation and development it's called Private Label. Make sure you (they) know the difference.

11. **Testing pH** - Most facilities are capable of pH testing. Find out if it is part of the initial consultation and recipe development or is an additional cost.

12. **Nutritional testing** - Some states and providences may require this before the bottles leave the facility. This should be included in the costs but ask.

13. **What is the minimum order?** - This will most likely be provided without asking and is very common. A facility won't go out of their way for a couple bottles but maybe a couple cases.

14. **Is sampling provided?** - It is standard operation to test your sauce throughout production but inquire how many times before you sign off.

15. **Can I provide my own ingredients?** - Grow your own product for your own hot sauce? It all depends on the co-packing if they want to accept outside product or not.

Bottle Your Own

Method	Financial risk	Legal Obligation
On Demand	Low	Medium
Drop Shipping	Medium	Medium
Private Label	Low	Low
Co-Packing	Medium	Low
Bottle Your Own	High	High

Bottling your own hot requires YOU to own, rent, lease, borrow, or use kitchen space or a manufacturing facility that has been inspected and approved for production

Bottling Your Own hot sauce is a deeply committed business endeavor but can be the most rewarding business model and can also produce the highest return on investment.

Bottling your own hot sauce requires owning, renting, or leasing an establishment where the sauce will be manufactured. This includes ALL the legal entities associated with inspections and approvals through agencies authorizing your facility to produce hot sauce.

Labeling requirements

Although graphic design of a label and logo can be as much fun as inventing a hot sauce the FDA has food labeling guidelines, but they do not approve labels.

FDA label guidelines

Every food product available for sale in the US follows these guidelines and they can be very stringent.

If your product has misinformation about its content, you could be subject to audits, fines and legal penalties and this could lead to the shutdown of operations. This mostly adheres to the nutritional label contents, but the display label will also have guidelines to follow as well.

How do I know what is in my hot sauce?

Your sauce will need to be sent to a laboratory for testing so that the nutritional contents can be displayed on the label per FDA guidelines. Typically, these laboratories will send a report giving the nutritional facts for your records and this is what will go on your nutritional label.

Once you have protected your recipe, found a kitchen to operate out of, and have followed FDA guidelines for labeling you are now ready for legal sales of your product. Deciding a price point and marketing to a specific audience are going to drive the sales of your product.

The importance of labeling a hot sauce correctly

Correctly labeling a hot sauce is directly related to successfully selling hot sauce. The FDA needs your hot sauce bottles to have the correct labeling per their guidelines. The FDA has a clear and precise guide to properly labeling your hot sauce for the display label and nutrition label as well. Most labeling companies know the FDA requirements.

Many local jurisdictions will also require specific labeling requirements but many of these requirements will be like what the FDA requires. Most states that accept hot sauce as a cottage food also require a statement that states the sauce is made without an inspection of the facility it is manufactured in.

You can also get a good idea of what needs to be on your label by reading any packaged hot sauce label off the shelf of your local grocery store. The FDA does not preapprove labels for food products so you will not have to submit them. However, your product could be subject to audits where your sauce will require testing (at your expense) and you may also need to provide other documentation as well.

Labels are also necessary for consumers to understand what your product is, what ingredients are used in it and other important information for food consumption. Your customers rely on these labels so be as truthful as possible.

How to add a bar code to your hot sauce

There isn't anything, stated anywhere, that says you need a bar code or UPC to sell hot sauce...but you do.

To obtain a bar code you will need a company name, a product name and other business information such as address and phone number. A barcode can be purchased for $30.00 for a single product but multiple bar codes will be needed for the same product available in different sizes. Barcodes are needed to identify product brands, to display pricing when scanned, and for tracking product inventory. Most retailers will require a bar code on the product label.

A UPC Bar Code (Universal Product Code) can be obtained from GS1 US and they have an easy-to-use web site that includes an estimator for the number of labels you will need if you have multiple products. For example, you make a hot sauce from one recipe, but the product comes in three different sizes. You will need three different bar codes for each of these products and this will increase costs.

UPC bar codes are not a random set of lines and numbers but are a selection of lines and code to produce data when scanned. They are used to display specific product data such as the name of the product, the price and size.

GS1 US is the authority that set the barcode standards for international commerce as well as e commerce.

What do I need to get a bar code?

To get a bar code you need a company name, a brand name, and a product description. You will also need to provide company information such as phone number, address and email contact so be prepared with this information when you apply.

Have your credit card information on hand. Address, phone number and credit card are common exchange of information for online purchases but don't scramble at the last minute with company name, brand name and product description.

Provide a company name, brand name and product description

Before you click any of the links below to apply for a bar code for your latest hot sauce creation, have your information such as company name, brand name and product description pre-selected. If you have gotten to the point of applying for a bar code then you must already have a great tasting sauce, some assimilation of a company and a location where it is being manufactured.

Don't scratch your head in the moment wondering what you are going to call your sauce because this information cannot be changed...you will have to create another new bar code.

Company name

This is the legal name of your business such as a DBA, LLC, or Sole Proprietorship, not the name of your hot sauce or web site. A domain name is the online presence of the company and is often different than the company name. A sole proprietorship is the easiest and most common type of business entity, and you can always migrate to a DBA or LLC.

You can use your name as the company name and do business as a sole proprietorship but not many companies associate their name with their brand of hot sauce. An EIN, DBA or LLC to protect your business but you don't need one to obtain a bar code for your hot sauce.

Brand name

A brand name is the name that stands out on the product label and is used to identify the product or product line. This is information that will display when your hot sauce's bar code is scanned. An example of this would be Franks RedHot manufactured by McCormick and Co. Franks would be the brand name and is globally recognized as a great tasing hot sauce.

Brand name can be a unique and catchy title used to

market your hot sauce. Extravagant and humorous names are used all the time as hot sauce brand names. This cannot be changed once you have a bar code so if your brand does, you will need to purchase another bar code.

Product description

You do not need a list of the ingredients of your hot sauce to get a bar code. That is included on the nutritional label. You will however need to describe the sauce as being hot, mild, medium and/or a brief description that includes what it is made with. Example: *A medium heat jalapeno and tomato salsa.*

You should obtain a DBA or LLC to conduct business, but you don't need one. The idea of obtaining a bar code is to sell hot sauce. A sole Proprietorship will be fine. **Don't decide on a company name, brand name and product name on the spur of the moment.** A sole proprietorship does not need to register with the state to conduct business. Many people in the hot sauce business begin with a sole proprietorship and obtain an EIN or use their social security number for tax purposes.

Phone number, address

This will be the lines of communication. This does not need to be a business location but needs to be a legal address. This information can be business or personal, but it will be time consuming and burdensome to continually change it.

How much does it cost to get a bar code?

A bar code costs about $30.00 for each individual product. This pricing will change as you purchase multiple labels but there is no renewal fee for the bar code. This cost will increase with every new product or every variation of a product, including size. The savings are only noticed after purchasing 10 or more bar codes.

If you plan on launching multiple products, then a GS1 Company Prefix will save you much more money. The annual cost for a company prefix is $250.00 for 10 barcodes. Purchasing 10 barcodes with just the GTIN would be $300.00. The cost savings would increase significantly upon purchasing hundreds or thousands of bar codes.

Where do I get a bar code for my hot sauce?

GS1 US GTIN (Global Trade Item Number) is a low-cost way of launching a new product. GTIN (pronounced G - Tin) are the numbers below the vertical lines of a bar code. A UPC are the lines above the numbers. The GTIN along with the UPC bar code can be used anywhere in the world.

Is the bar code created for me or do I need to create it?

GS1 Company Prefix is more cost effective for a company that has multiple products. It is not unusual for a hot sauce company to have many similar products listed under one brand or several sizes of the same product available. If your hot sauce comes in three sizes 5 oz, 10 oz and 12 oz, then you need three bar codes for the same product, not one.

Can I change the information of the bar code?

You can certainly add information about your product through the GS1 US Data Hub but shouldn't alter it. If your product changes in any way a new bar code will need to be purchased.

What does a barcode do?

A barcode is a pattern of elements that represent characters that a machine can read. The barcode is used by retailers to display product information when it is scanned. A UPC code is universally recognized and functions throughout the world. There is also a European code (EC).

Why do I need a bar code for my hot sauce?

You only need a barcode if you plan on selling hot sauce on a national or international level. Local retailers may not require one and if you plan on selling at farmers markets or your own retail store you shouldn't need one there either.

These types of venues are a great opportunity to introduce a new product line without investing hundreds of dollars on marketing, fancy packaging and multiple bar codes. However, it does give the hot sauce a professional and polished appearance.

This is another step toward your hot sauce having a professional and marketable appearance from the outside in. Many manufacturers include the UPC along with the nutritional label and the PDL in one label because a hot sauce label is so small.

Online retailers like Amazon, and many retailers globally will also require a product UPC barcode as part of the packaging label if you plan on selling through these portals. Amazon represents one third of all e commerce and is an excellent opportunity to sell hot sauce.

Is a bar code part of the Product Label Display?

A bar code is separate from a product label display and is usually on the back of a hot sauce bottle either horizontally or vertically depending on the size of the bottle. It will be below or next to or part of the nutritional label as one applied label. A Product Display Label (PDL) is the main label that shows the name of the product, a logo and other specific information.

Typically, the bar code, PDL and nutritional label are all part of one physical label as it is attached to a bottle of hot sauce. This makes it easier for printing and manufacturing. Most product labeling companies can combine the bar code, PDL and nutritional information into one product label that will fit your individual hot sauce bottles.

Does the FDA regulate bar codes?

The FDA does not require, regulate, or have a bar code requirements for product labels on hot sauce. They do require a nutritional label, ingredient list, weight, manufacturers address, and product display label.

How long does a bar code last?

You will need to change the bar code if the ingredients change. **If you are selling another hot sauce product under the same label...that is illegal!**

Print black lines on white spaces

UPC bar codes are meant to be scanned so that computer systems can quickly display date. Don't print the bar code in red because a scanner will not be able to read them. Other colors will not work as well as black either. The best colors for a bar code are black lines with a white background. However, there are other colors available that may blend in with your product label.

Size matters

It is not unusual for hot sauce to be available in 5 oz or even 3 oz bottles. Take this into consideration when planning the label of such a small bottle. The PDL and nutritional label can be minimized but the bar code needs to remain the same size and shouldn't be altered.

Don't change the size of the bar code

Changing the size of the bar code will also interfere with

its ability to be scanned properly. GS1 US will also tell you not to truncate it or alter it in any way. This will interfere with the quick scan ability of a UPC bar code.

What else does a bar code do

A bar code will give your product a unique identification not like any other product. This unique identifier can be searched in search engines.

What if the price of my hot sauce goes up?

If any part of your hot sauce alters, changes or differs from the product that was original to the bar code, than you will need a new one. Take this into consideration if your sauce becomes "new and improved" or if there are other marketing reasons for changing your original recipe.

Selling hot sauce from the start

The truth is... even an outstanding, award-winning hot sauce will not sell itself. Any product, whether it is following the wave of trends in hot sauce or not, will need to be promoted and marketed.

The legalities of marketing hot sauce

By the way...hot sauce doesn't sell itself and will usually need a lot of promotion and marketing. A strong marketing campaign will usually take an aggressive approach to presenting a product to customers, but it also needs to include the truth about the hot sauce.

Illegal marketing refers to activities that violate laws and regulations governing advertising and promotional practices. These activities can harm consumers, competitors, and the marketplace in general. Illegal marketing practices are typically subject to legal action by regulatory bodies, and companies engaging in such activities may face fines, legal penalties, and damage to their reputation. Here are some examples of illegal marketing practices.

False Advertising

Making false or misleading claims about a product or service. This can include false statements about the product's features, benefits, or performance.

Deceptive Marketing

Using deceptive tactics to mislead consumers. This might involve creating a false impression about the nature of the product or service, its price, or the terms of sale.

Unfair Competition

Engaging in practices that are considered unfair to competitors or that undermine the competitive marketplace. This could include spreading false information about competitors or engaging in anti-competitive behavior.

Bait-and-Switch

Advertising a product at a low price to attract customers and then attempting to upsell them to a more expensive item. This practice is deceptive and can be illegal.

Privacy Violations

Violating privacy laws by using unauthorized personal information for marketing purposes without consent. This includes practices such as spamming, phishing, or unauthorized data collection.

Unsolicited Communications

Sending unsolicited emails, text messages, or phone calls for marketing purposes without the recipient's consent may violate anti-spam laws.

Price Gouging

Charging excessively high prices for goods or services during emergencies or disasters, taking advantage of consumers in vulnerable situations.

Pyramid Schemes

Engaging in pyramid or Ponzi schemes where the primary source of profit is based on recruiting new members rather than on the sale of goods or services.

Counterfeit Products

 Marketing and selling counterfeit or fake products, which can infringe on intellectual property rights and deceive consumers.

Violation of Consumer Protection Laws

Breaking any laws or regulations designed to protect consumers, such as those related to product safety, warranty, or consumer rights.

It's important for businesses to be aware of and comply with applicable laws and regulations related to marketing and advertising. Regulatory bodies, such as the Federal Trade Commission (FTC) in the United States, are responsible for enforcing these laws and acting against companies engaged in illegal marketing practices. Companies that engage in ethical and legal marketing build trust with consumers and contribute to a fair and competitive marketplace.

There are many ethical decisions to make in the decisions that need to be made to market your product and there are also legal implications behind selling your product honestly. According to Forbes there are several illegal marketing practices that should not be pursued. Insider info and bait and switch marketing campaigns are illegal, and it is easy to get involved.

Insider info

Yes, using insider information in marketing can be illegal, particularly if it involves non-public, material information that could influence trading decisions or provide an unfair advantage to certain individuals or entities. Insider information generally refers to confidential information about a company that has not been disclosed to the public and, if known, could impact the company's stock value or influence investment decisions.

The concept of insider trading is most commonly associated with securities and financial markets, but the principles extend to various aspects of business, including marketing. If individuals within a company use non-public information for marketing purposes, such as making promotional decisions or crafting advertising strategies based on undisclosed financial data, customer information, or upcoming product releases, it could be considered unethical and potentially illegal.

Legal issues

Securities Laws

In the context of publicly traded companies, using insider information for marketing purposes could violate securities laws. The U.S. Securities and Exchange Commission (SEC) and similar regulatory bodies in other countries have regulations against insider trading.

Fair Trading Practices

Unfairly using insider information in marketing may be considered an unfair trade practice. It can lead to an uneven playing field in the marketplace and harm competitors who do not have access to the same confidential information.

Corporate Governance and Ethical Standards

Companies typically have internal policies and codes of conduct that prohibit the misuse of insider information. Violating these standards can result in disciplinary action, including termination of employment.

Reputation and Trust

Engaging in marketing practices based on insider information can damage a company's reputation and erode trust among stakeholders, including customers, investors, and partners.

It's crucial for individuals involved in marketing or any other business activities to be aware of the legal and ethical implications of using non-public information. Companies often provide training on these matters to ensure that employees understand the importance of compliance with laws and ethical standards.

If you have concerns or questions about the legality of certain marketing practices, it is advisable to consult legal professionals who specialize in securities law and business ethics for guidance tailored to your specific situation and jurisdiction.

Product misconception

Deceptive advertising and the ability to substantiate claims are also cause for legal implications against on the way you are marketing your product. Health claims such as "zero calorie" or "contains vitamin C" may be truthful and evident on the nutritional label. Claims such as "improves digestion" may not.

Penalties for illegal marketing

The penalties for illegal marketing can vary depending on the nature and severity of the violation, as well as the jurisdiction in which the offense occurs. Regulatory bodies and government agencies enforce laws related to marketing, and they may impose a range of penalties to deter and punish illegal practices. Some common penalties for illegal marketing include:

Fines

Companies found guilty of illegal marketing practices may be subject to fines. The amount of the fine can vary widely based on factors such as the nature of the violation, the scale of the offense, and the jurisdiction.

Civil Lawsuits

Individuals or entities affected by illegal marketing may file civil lawsuits seeking damages. This can result in financial compensation being awarded to the injured parties.

Injunctions

Regulatory bodies may seek court orders to stop the

offending company from continuing the illegal marketing practices. Injunctions can be issued to halt specific activities or to require compliance with certain regulations.

Corrective Advertising

In some cases, companies may be required to engage in corrective advertising to rectify the false or misleading information they have disseminated.

Revocation of Licenses or Permits

If a business holds licenses or permits related to its operations, regulatory authorities may have the power to revoke or suspend these licenses in response to illegal marketing practices.

Criminal Penalties

Serious violations may lead to criminal charges, particularly in cases of fraud or intentional deception. Individuals involved in illegal marketing practices could face fines, probation, or even imprisonment.

Reputation Damage

Beyond legal penalties, companies engaging in illegal marketing may suffer significant damage to their reputation. Negative publicity and loss of trust among consumers can have long-lasting effects on a business.

Ban from Advertising

In some cases, regulatory bodies may ban a company or individual from engaging in specific types of advertising for a certain period.

Compliance Monitoring

Regulatory authorities may require the company to implement compliance monitoring measures to ensure they adhere to marketing regulations in the future.

It's crucial for businesses to understand and comply with marketing laws and regulations to avoid these penalties. The specific legal framework and enforcement mechanisms vary by country and region, so companies should be aware of the rules applicable to their operations. Seeking legal advice and staying informed about updates to marketing regulations can help businesses mitigate the risk of engaging in illegal marketing practices.

Other legal actions taken for selling hot sauce

Now that you have protected your hot sauce recipe, found a kitchen that has passed health inspections, it is now time to promote and sell your hot sauce. If you have followed some of the principles above, you should have some important steps covered but there are a few more that will make your business more professional.

File a DBA or LLC

A DBA (Doing Business As) is filed on the state or county level and will generally cost about $35.00 but not every state has a DBA filing requirement. This DBA is simply a fictitious name that you are operating under. It could be the name of your sauce or a name you have chosen for the company making the sauce.

Verify that the name of your sauce or company is unique and has not been taken. The last thing that you want to do is come up with a great name for your sauce only to find it has already been taken. This could be different from your DBA or website name. The name of your sauce should stand alone and not have any similarities to other brands of sauce. You may want the name of the business (DBA), the website and the hot sauce to all have the same name but it is not necessary.

This is also true of a logo and label. A logo is a trademark and cannot be legally used by another company once it has been registered. Designing a logo can be fun but it needs to be unique, stand alone and attract consumers. Use the TESS link to verify a logo design but chances are if you designed it yourself...it's probably unique.

Federal ID or Social Security Number

Getting an EIN is as simple as applying here with the IRS and can be done in a matter of minutes. There is no cost for registering but this will be a requirement once you begin earning an income and will need to file business tax returns.

Get insured

Insurance is an important part of starting a hot sauce business in order to protect your assets, protection against lawsuits or accidents. Insurance for startup business can be obtain for under $30.00 a month.

Get a bank account

Opening a bank account will be necessary once money starts to change hands. You do not need a business account or a business credit card, but this is a good way to keep expenses separate. This is not a legal issue, but it is certainly needed for making money transactions.

Making delicious hot sauce is easy compared to some of the necessary steps needed to sell hot sauce legally. If you are planning on making and selling hot sauce from a startup business and through entrepreneurship into a successful commercial hot sauce company…than you need to know the legal matters.

If you have a great hot sauce recipe, bottled it in an approved kitchen and provided a product and nutritional label…you are now ready to sell your sauce. There are many opportunities to begin selling hot sauce which little or no investment.

The business side of things

Starting a hot sauce company can be very exciting and fun but there are many things on the business side that may not be as fun as making new hot sauce creations.

It is the set up to open and run a legitimate business that is absolutely necessary. There are many legal operations with running a hot sauce business once you have established it.

Starting a hot sauce business involves several legal considerations to ensure compliance with local, state, and federal regulations. Here are the general steps you might need to take to legally start a hot sauce business:

Business Plan

Develop a comprehensive business plan outlining your hot sauce business, including your target market, marketing strategy, pricing, distribution plan, and financial projections.

Business Structure

Choose a legal structure for your business, such as a sole proprietorship, partnership, limited liability company (LLC), or corporation. The structure you choose will affect aspects like liability, taxes, and regulatory requirements.

Business Registration

Register your business with the appropriate authorities. This may involve registering your business name and obtaining a business license from your local city or county government.

Food Safety Regulations

Comply with food safety regulations to ensure that your hot sauce is produced and handled in a safe manner. This may include operating from a commercial kitchen that meets health and safety standards.

Labeling Compliance

Ensure that your hot sauce labels comply with food labeling regulations. Include information such as ingredients, nutritional facts, allergens, and any required health or safety warnings.

FDA Registration

If you plan to sell your hot sauce across state lines in the United States, register your food facility with the U.S.

Food and Drug Administration (FDA). Even if you operate within one state, compliance with federal regulations is often necessary.

State and Local Permits

Obtain necessary permits from state and local health departments. This may include food handler permits, food establishment permits, and other relevant licenses.

Insurance

Consider getting liability insurance to protect your business in case of product-related issues or other liabilities. Insurance can provide coverage for legal expenses and damages.

Supplier Compliance

Ensure that your suppliers, if any, comply with food safety standards. This is especially important if you source ingredients from external suppliers.

Distribution Agreements

If you plan to distribute your hot sauce through retailers or other channels, establish distribution agreements that outline terms, pricing, and any legal responsibilities.

Intellectual Property

Consider trademarking your hot sauce brand and logo to protect your intellectual property. Conduct a thorough search to ensure your chosen name and branding elements are not already in use.

Tax Compliance

Register for any necessary state and federal taxes, including sales tax. Keep accurate financial records and comply with tax reporting requirements.

Environmental Regulations

Be aware of and comply with any environmental regulations related to your hot sauce production process, waste disposal, and other relevant factors.

Marketing Compliance

Ensure that your marketing materials, including online content and advertising, comply with relevant laws and regulations to avoid issues related to false advertising or deceptive practices.

Consulting with legal professionals, such as attorneys specializing in food law, can provide valuable guidance tailored to your specific location and business model. It's essential to stay informed about regulatory changes and to maintain a commitment to food safety and compliance throughout the operation of your hot sauce business.

Employees

Hiring employees to help with operations of a hot sauce business will have many legal obligations that will parallel any business structure.

Can you sell hot sauce...illegally?

You can sell homemade hot sauce made from an uninspected kitchen to someone else without much legal implications. It is a lot like selling any item off of Craigslist or through garage sales. However, like many things in business, there are some ethical issues associated with selling a product which may not have gone through stringent sanitation practices.

Chances are, if you sell a few bottles of your homemade hot sauce to your neighbor there will not be any fines on the state or federal level. The authorities pursuing illegal trade of goods has larger cases.

Penalties

Like anything related to selling hot sauce on a global level, the severity of the fines or penalties can vary significantly.

However, selling hot sauce on a small scale without the proper licensing will usually only result in fines without an arrest warrant, incarceration, or further legal actions. You could probably get away with selling hot sauce to a few friends without any consequences…but you didn't here that from me!

Selling hot sauce online

Selling hot sauce online requires the same licensing and permits as selling it directly to consumers. The regulations will follow the requirements set by the region in which your business is set up.

Selling product beyond the shelf-life date

In the US, the federal government does not require a food expiration date on hot sauce labels. These labels are generally supplied by manufacturers to communicate to consumers the freshness of their products.

What if a consumer is harmed by an expired hot sauce?

Civil lawsuits can be filed against manufacturers if there is harm caused to a consumer for eating an expired hot sauce. On the plus side…many hot sauce products have a shelf life of many months or even years.

Selling food products beyond their shelf-life date can be illegal and pose risks to consumer health. The shelf-life date, often indicated as the "expiration date" or "best before date," is a critical aspect of food safety and quality assurance. It is set by manufacturers based on factors like the product's ingredients, processing methods, packaging, and storage conditions.

Here are some key points to consider ethical considerations for labeling a hot sauce with the proper expiration date.

Regulatory Compliance

In many jurisdictions, selling food products beyond their stated shelf-life date is a violation of food safety regulations. Regulatory bodies, such as the Food and Drug Administration (FDA) in the United States or the European Food Safety Authority (EFSA) in Europe, establish guidelines and regulations regarding shelf life and product dating.

Consumer Protection

Selling expired or spoiled food products can harm consumers and erode trust in your brand. It may lead to legal action, negative publicity, and damage to your business reputation.

Labeling Compliance

Ensure that your food product labels accurately reflect the shelf life information and adhere to labeling regulations. Misleading or incorrect labeling can result in legal consequences.

Health Risks

Beyond legal considerations, selling food products past their shelf-life date poses health risks. The quality and safety of the product may deteriorate over time, leading to spoilage, bacterial contamination, or other issues.

Product Liability

If consumers experience illness or harm due to consuming expired products, you could face product liability claims. This can result in legal action and financial repercussions for your business.

To comply with legal and ethical standards, it's essential to:

Monitor Inventory

Regularly check and rotate your inventory to ensure that products with earlier expiration dates are sold or removed from shelves first.

Dispose of Expired Products

Safely dispose of products that have passed their shelf life date and are no longer fit for consumption.

Follow Storage Guidelines

Adhere to recommended storage conditions for your products to maximize their shelf life.

Stay Informed

Keep abreast of food safety regulations and guidelines relevant to your industry and location.

Always consult with legal professionals and local health authorities to ensure that you are in compliance with food safety regulations and that your business practices align with industry standards. Ignoring these guidelines can lead to serious legal consequences and damage to your business reputation.

How to determine the shelf life

Many types of hot sauce can have a longer expiration date than many other condiments used to enhance certain foods. This is true because of the acidity or low pH value of many varieties of hot sauce. Determining when a hot sauce is no longer acceptable for consumption and stamping it with an expiration date is up to the manufacturer.

How to determine the expiration date of hot sauce

As a general rule, determining the expiration date of a hot sauce can be done with laboratory testing to

determine the rate of bacterial growth. The expiration date should then be labeled on a hot sauce bottle to communicate to consumers the quality of the sauce over a duration of time.

A manufacturer or producer of a hot sauce does not want a consumer eating a hot sauce that has spoiled and does not taste good anymore. This could cause harm to the human body and will give a negative portrayal of the food product. Therefore, a date is stamped on the product by the manufacturer as a communication tool to let consumers know it should not be eaten after that date.

These dates are also used as a way to cut down on food waste. If a consumer does not know how long a product is considered edible, they are more likely to dispose of it, therefore wasting a product that is still edible. Consumers may not be aware of the longevity of some brands of hot sauce, especially if they do not eat it regularly.

Manufacturing companies perform tests, either within their companies or by outside agencies, on their products to determine the expiration date of a hot sauce. The tests performed will put hot sauce through different temperature settings, exposure to light, and other conditions a product may go through during storage and consumption.

The hot sauce is then tested to determine if the quality is still OK for consumption or edible after a certain period. Hot sauce can be tested for longer durations compared to other products to determine the quality of the product over time. The hot sauce should not be consumed during these periods of testing for reasons that it may have spoiled. Once the expiration date is determined it is labeled on the nutritional label or onto the glass but there may be different phrases used on products to differentiate sales or consumption.

The expiration date is different from the "sell by" date

According to FSIS (Food Safety and Inspection Service), the "sell by" date is used to communicate to stores selling the product as a recommendation for how long to display the product on store shelves. The expiration date or "use by" date is intended for the consumer to be aware of how long the product will last for consumption and may be different from the "sell by" date.

How to tell if the hot sauce has gone bad

Many varieties of hot sauce have a low pH giving them a long-extended shelf life so they will still taste good. Therefore, it won't be as obvious that the sauce has gone bad when compared to other condiments. There are simple sensory testing methods involving sight and scent that can be used without elaborate or expensive laboratory testing. This should be done with any hot sauces you intend to have for sale and could take months or years for some sauces.

Visual inspection

There are ways to determine if a hot sauce has gone bad that does not take any kind of scientific experimenting or expensive laboratory testing. It's not rocket science to look at a bottle of hot sauce to see mold or bacteria growth. If this were the case this would be a very, very old hot sauce or a sauce with a higher alkaline level.

It is not uncommon to have some popular well-selling brands of hot sauce separate over time. Some solids can sink to the bottom, but this is not an indication that the sauce has gone bad. This is very common and is why hot sauces are labeled "shake well before serving".

Further visual testing can be done over time to compare the sauce being tested to freshly made sauce over specific increments of time. This test can compare color, texture, and mold growth against a sauce that has been determined to be fresh.

Smell

Testing the scent of a hot sauce would be like a visual test and may not be quite as noticeable as a visual test if the sauce is bad. Hot sauces can have a sharp pungent scent or almost sour scent if the sauce has a high vinegar content.

Also like the visual test, using a sense of smell will be more prominent on a sauce that is on the alkaline side of the pH scale. Milk and cheeses can shorten the shelf life or push a hot sauce towards the alkaline side of the scale, making the "smell test" more noticeable. Fortunately, many hot sauces do not contain these ingredients.

Microbiological testing

Microbiological testing is the testing of bacteria, mold, or pathogenic organisms in a hot sauce within a controlled laboratory setting. This type of testing is essential for food safety, but these test results can cost over $500 per product.

These manufacturing companies hire laboratories to test for shelf life such as RL Food Laboratory. Some will only test for a duration of one year, but many hot sauces will last longer. Many of these labs perform accelerated testing to mimic a longer duration and provide an extended date. The food testing laboratories will store the products in conditions like what people may have in their homes and perform periodic testing.

Don't taste

The last thing you will want to do is taste a hot sauce that has gone bad. Not only will it be foul-tasting, but it could also upset your stomach and make you sick. Larger companies may perform more elaborate testing than simply tasting a sauce.

However, no one knows your hot sauce as much as you do. This could prove to have accurate results for sensory testing but is not an indication of bacterial growth unless you can see it. If you are confident in a taste test to determine an expiration date for your hot sauce, perform some simple sensory testing first.

How long does hot sauce last once it is opened?

Opened hot sauce can last up to 6 months in a non-refrigerated environment. Hot sauce that has been opened and refrigerated can last 1 to 2 years. Hot sauces containing fruits may have a shorter shelf life if the pH isn't low and a cream-based hot sauce will only have a shelf life of about 2 weeks once it is opened.

How to extend the shelf life of a hot sauce

The shelf life of a hot sauce can be extended by adding vinegar or preservatives. Vinegar is one of the most common components of a hot sauce and many preservatives used are natural as well. The addition of vinegar will alter the recipe if the hot sauce does not already contain it.

Distilled white vinegar will be more acidic than many other types such as apple cider vinegar or rice wine vinegar but they won't affect the expiration date by much.

Some common preservatives such sodium benzoate, sorbate, and citric acid are used specifically in a hot sauce that does not have a low pH. These preservatives, also commonly used in other condiments, increase shelf life but not as much as vinegar may.

Other methods of extending the shelf life of a hot sauce once it is opened would be to make sure the cap is on tight and sealed properly. Allowing air to enter will promote bacterially and mold growth. Also, there can be dried sauce on the inside of the lid or cap that promotes bacterial growth. Keep the cap and top of the bottle clean.

Does the pH of hot sauce change over time?

An expiration date is not required by federal regulations. Labeling a hot with an expiration date or stamping it with "best used by" date is not under USDA, FDA, or other federal regulations. However, the FDA does consider determining the product's shelf life as part of the manufacturer's responsibility.

This is the reason many manufactures do not put the "best if used by" date on their hot sauces, because it is another step and expense in the manufacturing process, especially for smaller operations.

Why put it on the label?

If you plan on providing your hot sauce with an expiration date the USDA under the jurisdiction of the FSIS (Food Safety Inspection Services) recommends that manufacturers provide a "best if used by" date on products in efforts to help reduce food waste.

Adding the expiration date on a hot sauce bottle keeps consumers from guessing if the sauce is still edible or not. Most may not realize the extended shelf life of many hot sauces and discard before the product has gone bad. Labeling shows the last date of the peak quality, and this keeps consumers from wasting food before it has gone bad. Because labeling can be a different part of the production and are ordered in larger quantities the bottling sauce, the dates are often stamped on the glass bottle.

Stamped on glass

Often the expiration date is stamped on the glass and not printed on the label. Simple handheld stamps can be purchased or larger production operations may require machines. This will give a bottled hot sauce a professional appearance and will communicate to consumers the manufacturer's desire to provide the consumer with a fresh product.

The ink should have a contrasting color from the glass (or plastic) bottle and there needs to be a certain type of ink used. Typically, a quick-dry ink supplied by the manufacturer of the stamp must be used. Ink would need to be loaded much like an inkjet printer.

Printing an expiration date on glass bottles using a handheld Reiner Jetstamp 790 MP or 792 MP will require a lot of handling. It will also require additional handling and maintenance of equipment. Take this into consideration before committing to stamping your hot sauce bottles with an expiration date.

Handheld printer

There is a variety of handheld printers suitable for printing on glass bottles available for under $300. Hand-held operations can be set up to be done without handling every bottle and speed up the stamping process.

Why isn't the expiration date on the label?

Hot sauce may be bottled and packaged in precise amounts based on the number of sales a business may make. The labels are often produced separately and are purchased in large quantities because there isn't expiration to them.

Therefore you may have 1,000 labels but only 100 bottles of hot sauce that would have the same expiration. You could have 900 labels with the expiration date labeled on them just lying around until your next anticipated sale.

How long does hot sauce last?

On average some hot sauces with high acidity or pH level below 4.6 can last for 2 to 3 years if kept in the right conditions. Hot sauces that use vinegar get preserved from the acidic contents of the vinegar to increase the longevity of the sauce.

Typically, a hot sauce will be labeled as a "best by" date much **BEFORE** it extends past the recommended date. This is a tactic used by the manufacturer to guarantee freshness.

Can you use hot sauce after the expiration date?

As a general rule, you should not consume hot sauce after the expiration date stamped on the bottle or packaging. Manufacturers of food products put a "best if used" date on a bottle of hot sauce to keep the consumer from eating a product that is not fresh. The manufacturer knows the product better than anyone and they certainly do not want to provide low-quality products.

I examined the expiration date of 50 top-selling hot sauce brands to determine what the average expiration date of hot sauce is or if they have an expiration date on the label.

A simple Louisiana style hot sauce consisting of hot peppers, vinegar, salt, and garlic has the longest expiration date among many different types of sauces.

Taxes

Taxes will need to be paid on good sold... no matter if you are selling at a large commercial scale or at a farmer's market.

Paying taxes on goods sold is a crucial aspect of conducting business and is subject to the tax regulations of the jurisdiction in which the business operates. This can get a young business in trouble if you do not fully grasp how taxes are paid BEFORE business begins.

A hot sauce business is subject to taxes, including income taxes, sales taxes, and possibly other local or state taxes. The specific tax obligations can vary based on the location and nature of the business. If you need more detailed information, I can look up specific tax requirements for hot sauce businesses in a particular location.

The hot sauce business typically pays taxes based on its legal structure. For example, if it's a sole proprietorship or a partnership, the business taxes are usually paid as part of the owner's personal tax return. If the business is set up as a corporation or LLC, it will have its own tax return and will pay taxes separately from the owners. The specific tax forms and requirements can vary based on the business's location and structure. If you need more detailed information on this topic, I can look up specific tax payment procedures for hot sauce businesses.

The process generally involves several key components:

Sales Tax or Value Added Tax (VAT)

Many jurisdictions impose a sales tax or VAT on the sale
of goods. This tax is usually a percentage of the sale price
and is collected by the seller on behalf of the government.
The tax rate and regulations vary widely between
countries and regions.

Sales Tax Registration

Businesses that meet certain criteria may be required to
register for a sales tax or VAT number with the tax
authorities. This registration allows the business to collect
taxes on behalf of the government.

Tax Collection at Point of Sale

When a business sells goods, it typically includes the
applicable sales tax or VAT in the total price paid by the
customer. The business is then responsible for segregating
and reporting this tax amount separately.

Record Keeping

Businesses are required to maintain accurate records of
their sales, including the amount of tax collected. This
documentation is essential for tax reporting purposes and
may be subject to audit by tax authorities.

Filing Tax Returns

Periodically, businesses are required to file tax returns with the relevant tax authorities. These returns detail the sales made, taxes collected, and any eligible deductions. The frequency of filing can vary, such as monthly, quarterly, or annually.

Payment of Taxes

After filing the tax returns, the business is obligated to remit the collected taxes to the tax authorities. This payment is typically made electronically or by submitting a check along with the tax return.

Penalties for Non-Compliance

Failure to comply with tax regulations, such as not collecting or remitting the correct amount of taxes, can result in penalties and fines. Therefore, it is essential for businesses to stay informed about tax laws and fulfill their obligations accurately and on time.

International Considerations

For businesses engaged in international trade, additional considerations may arise, such as customs duties, import/export taxes, and compliance with the tax laws of multiple jurisdictions.

It's important for businesses to consult with tax professionals or accountants to ensure compliance with local tax laws and regulations, as these can vary significantly from one jurisdiction to another. Additionally, staying informed about changes in tax laws is crucial for adapting to new requirements and avoiding potential issues.

What happens if you don't pay taxes on goods sold?

Failure to pay taxes on goods sold can have serious consequences, as it is considered a violation of tax laws. The specific repercussions may vary depending on the jurisdiction and the severity of the non-compliance, but here are some common consequences:

Penalties and Interest

Tax authorities typically impose penalties for late or non-payment of taxes. These penalties can be a percentage of the unpaid taxes and may accrue over time. Interest charges may also apply to the overdue amount.

Seizure of Assets

In extreme cases of non-compliance, tax authorities may have the authority to seize assets to recover unpaid taxes. This could include physical assets such as inventory, equipment, or even bank accounts.

Legal Action

Tax authorities may take legal action against the business or individuals responsible for non-payment of taxes. This can involve court proceedings, fines, and other legal consequences.

Revocation of Business Licenses

Some jurisdictions have the authority to revoke or suspend business licenses for non-compliance with tax obligations. This can severely impact the ability of a business to operate legally.

Criminal Charges

In cases of deliberate tax evasion or fraud, criminal charges may be filed against the responsible parties. This can lead to fines, imprisonment, or both.

Audits and Investigations

Tax authorities may conduct audits or investigations to examine a business's financial records and ensure compliance with tax laws. This process can be time-consuming and may result in additional penalties and fines if discrepancies are found.

Damage to Reputation

Non-compliance with tax laws can damage the reputation of a business. Customers, suppliers, and partners may lose trust in the business, and this can have long-term negative consequences.

It's important for businesses to prioritize compliance with tax obligations and seek professional advice if they have concerns or questions about their tax responsibilities. Ignoring or neglecting tax obligations can lead to significant financial and legal consequences.

Made in United States
Orlando, FL
15 October 2024

52685263R00059